Louis MacNeice was born in Belf;
Church of Ireland rector, later a bis.   ... ... in
England at Sherborne, Marlborough and Merton College,
Oxford. His first book of poems, *Blind Fireworks*,
appeared in 1929, and he subsequently worked as a
translator, literary critic, playwright, autobiographer, BBC
producer and feature writer. *The Burning Perch*, his last
volume of poems, appeared shortly before his death in
1963.

by Louis MacNeice

Collected Poems
Edited by E. R. Dodds

Selected Poems
Edited by Michael Longley

The Strings Are False:
An Unfinished Autobiography
Edited by E. R. Dodds

with W. H. Auden
Letters from Iceland

by Jon Stallworthy
Louis MacNeice:
A Biography

by Edna Longley
Louis MacNeice:
A Critical Study

LOUIS MACNEICE Autumn Journal

faber and faber

First published in 1939
by Faber and Faber Limited
Bloomsbury House
74-77 Great Russell Street
London WC1B 3DA

This paperback edition first published in 1998
Phototypeset by Parker Typesetting Service, Leicester.
Printed and bound in Great Britain by
TJ International Ltd, Padstow, Cornwall

A CIP record for this book
is available from the British Library

ISBN 978-0-571-19745-3

10 9 8 7 6 5 4 3

Note

I am aware that there are over-statements in this poem – e.g. in the passages dealing with Ireland, the Oxford by-election or my own more private existence. There are also inconsistencies. If I had been writing a didactic poem proper, it would have been my job to qualify or eliminate these over-statements and inconsistencies. But I was writing what I have called a Journal. In a journal or a personal letter a man writes what he feels at the moment; to attempt scientific truthfulness would be – paradoxically – dishonest. The truth of a lyric is different from the truths of science and this poem is something half-way between the lyric and the didactic poem. In as much as it is half-way towards a didactic poem I trust that it contains some 'criticism of life' or implies some standards which are not merely personal. I was writing it from August 1938 until the New Year and have not altered any passages relating to public events in the light of what happened after the time of writing. Thus the section about Barcelona having been written before the fall of Barcelona, I should consider it dishonest to have qualified it retrospectively by my reactions to the later event. Nor am I attempting to offer what so many people now demand from poets – a final verdict or a balanced judgment. It is the nature of this poem to be neither final nor balanced. I have certain beliefs which, I hope, emerge in the course of it but which I have refused to abstract from their context. For this reason I shall probably be called a trimmer by some and a sentimental extremist by others. But poetry in my opinion must be honest before anything else and I refuse to be 'objective' or clear-cut at the cost of honesty.

L. M.

March, 1939

AUTUMN JOURNAL

i

Close and slow, summer is ending in Hampshire,
  Ebbing away down ramps of shaven lawn where close-
    clipped yew
Insulates the lives of retired generals and admirals
  And the spyglasses hung in the hall and the prayer-
    books ready in the pew
And August going out to the tin trumpets of nasturtiums
  And the sunflowers' Salvation Army blare of brass
And the spinster sitting in a deck-chair picking up stitches
  Not raising her eyes to the noise of the 'planes that pass
Northward from Lee-on-Solent. Macrocarpa and cypress
  And roses on a rustic trellis and mulberry trees
And bacon and eggs in a silver dish for breakfast
  And all the inherited assets of bodily ease
And all the inherited worries, rheumatism and taxes,
  And whether Stella will marry and what to do with
    Dick
And the branch of the family that lost their money in
    Hatry
  And the passing of the *Morning Post* and of life's
    climacteric
And the growth of vulgarity, cars that pass the gate-lodge
  And crowds undressing on the beach
And the hiking cockney lovers with thoughts directed
  Neither to God nor Nation but each to each.
But the home is still a sanctum under the pelmets,
  All quiet on the Family Front,
Farmyard noises across the fields at evening
  While the trucks of the Southern Railway dawdle . . .
    shunt

Into poppy sidings for the night – night which knows no
      passion
   No assault of hands or tongue
For all is old as flint or chalk or pine-needles
   And the rebels and the young
Have taken the train to town or the two-seater
   Unravelling rails or road,
Losing the thread deliberately behind them –
   Autumnal palinode.
And I am in the train too now and summer is going
   South as I go north
Bound for the dead leaves falling, the burning bonfire,
   The dying that brings forth
The harder life, revealing the trees' girders,
   The frost that kills the germs of *laissez-faire*;
West Meon, Tisted, Farnham, Woking, Weybridge,
   Then London's packed and stale and pregnant air.
My dog, a symbol of the abandoned order,
   Lies on the carriage floor,
Her eyes inept and glamorous as a film star's,
   Who wants to live, i.e. wants more
Presents, jewellery, furs, gadgets, solicitations
   As if to live were not
Following the curve of a planet or controlled water
   But a leap in the dark, a tangent, a stray shot.
It is this we learn after so many failures,
   The building of castles in sand, of queens in snow,
That we cannot make any corner in life or in life's beauty,
   That no river is a river which does not flow.
Surbiton, and a woman gets in, painted
   With dyed hair but a ladder in her stocking and eyes
Patient beneath the calculated lashes,
   Inured for ever to surprise;

4

And the train's rhythm becomes the *ad nauseam* repetition
    Of every tired aubade and maudlin madrigal,
The faded airs of sexual attraction
    Wandering like dead leaves along a warehouse wall:
'I loved my love with a platform ticket,
    A jazz song,
A handbag, a pair of stockings of Paris Sand –
    I loved her long.
I loved her between the lines and against the clock,
    Not until death
But till life did us part I loved her with paper money
    And with whisky on the breath.
I loved her with peacock's eyes and the wares of Carthage,
    With glass and gloves and gold and a powder puff
With blasphemy, camaraderie, and bravado
    And lots of other stuff.
I loved my love with the wings of angels
    Dipped in henna, unearthly red,
With my office hours, with flowers and sirens,
    With my budget, my latchkey, and my daily bread.'
And so to London and down the ever-moving Stairs
Where a warm wind blows the bodies of men together
    And blows apart their complexes and cares.

Spider, spider, twisting tight –
   But the watch is wary beneath the pillow –
I am afraid in the web of night
   When the window is fingered by the shadows of
      branches,
When the lions roar beneath the hill
   And the meter clicks and the cistern bubbles
And the gods are absent and the men are still –
   Noli me tangere, my soul is forfeit.
Some now are happy in the hive of home,
   Thigh over thigh and a light in the night nursery,
And some are hungry under the starry dome
   And some sit turning handles.
Glory to God in the Lowest, peace beneath the earth,
   Dumb and deaf at the nadir;
I wonder now whether anything is worth
   The eyelid opening and the mind recalling.
And I think of Persephone gone down to dark,
   No more a virgin, gone the garish meadow,
But why must she come back, why must the snowdrop
      mark
   That life goes on for ever?
There are nights when I am lonely and long for love
   But to-night is quintessential dark forbidding
Anyone beside or below me; only above
   Pile high the tumulus, good-bye to starlight.
Good-bye the Platonic sieve of the Carnal Man
   But good-bye also Plato's philosophising;
I have a better plan
   To hit the target straight without circumlocution.

If you can equate Being in its purest form
    With denial of all appearance,
Then let me disappear – the scent grows warm
    For pure Not-Being, Nirvana.
Only the spider spinning out his reams
    Of colourless thread says Only there are always
Interlopers, dreams,
    Who let no dead dog lie nor death be final;
Suggesting, while he spins, that to-morrow will outweigh
    To-night, that Becoming is a match for Being,
That to-morrow is also a day,
    That I must leave my bed and face the music.
As all the others do who with a grin
    Shake off sleep like a dog and hurry to desk or engine
And the fear of life goes out as they clock in
    And history is reasserted.
Spider, spider, your irony is true;
    Who am I – or I – to demand oblivion?
I must go out to-morrow as the others do
    And build the falling castle;
Which has never fallen, thanks
    Not to any formula, red tape or institution,
Not to any creeds or banks,
    But to the human animal's endless courage.
Spider, spider, spin
    Your register and let me sleep a little,
Not now in order to end but to begin
    The task begun so often.

iii

August is nearly over, the people
   Back from holiday are tanned
With blistered thumbs and a wallet of snaps and a little
   Joie de vivre which is contraband;
Whose stamina is enough to face the annual
   Wait for the annual spree,
Whose memories are stamped with specks of sunshine
   Like faded *fleurs de lys*.
Now the till and the typewriter call the fingers,
   The workman gathers his tools
For the eight-hour day but after that the solace
   Of films or football pools
Or of the gossip or cuddle, the moments of self-glory
   Or self-indulgence, blinkers on the eyes of doubt,
The blue smoke rising and the brown lace sinking
   In the empty glass of stout.
Most are accepters, born and bred to harness,
   And take things as they come,
But some refusing harness and more who are refused it
   Would pray that another and a better Kingdom come,
Which now is sketched in the air or travestied in slogans
   Written in chalk or tar on stucco or plaster-board
But in time may find its body in men's bodies,
   Its law and order in their heart's accord,
Where skill will no longer languish nor energy be
      trammelled
   To competition and graft,
Exploited in subservience but not allegiance
   To an utterly lost and daft
System that gives a few at fancy prices

8

Their fancy lives
While ninety-nine in the hundred who never attend the
    banquet
Must wash the grease of ages off the knives.
And now the tempter whispers 'But you also
    Have the slave-owner's mind,
Would like to sleep on a mattress of easy profits,
    To snap your fingers or a whip and find
Servants or houris ready to wince and flatter
    And build with their degradation your self-esteem;
What you want is not a world of the free in function
    But a niche at the top, the skimmings of the cream.'
And I answer that that is largely so for habit makes me
    Think victory for one implies another's defeat,
That freedom means the power to order, and that in order
    To preserve the values dear to the élite
The élite must remain a few. It is so hard to imagine
    A world where the many would have their chance
        without
A fall in the standard of intellectual living
    And nothing left that the highbrow cared about.
Which fears must be suppressed. There is no reason for
        thinking
    That, if you give a chance to people to think or live,
The arts of thought or life will suffer and become rougher
    And not return more than you could ever give.
And now I relapse to sleep, to dreams perhaps and
        reaction
    Where I shall play the gangster or the sheikh,
Kill for the love of killing, make the world my sofa,
    Unzip the women and insult the meek.
Which fantasies no doubt are due to my private history,
    Matter for the analyst,

But the final cure is not in his past-dissecting fingers
  But in a future of action, the will and fist
Of those who abjure the luxury of self-pity
  And prefer to risk a movement without being sure
If movement would be better or worse in a hundred
  Years or a thousand when their heart is pure.
None of our hearts are pure, we always have mixed
    motives,
  Are self deceivers, but the worst of all
Deceits is to murmur 'Lord, I am not worthy'
  And, lying easy, turn your face to the wall.
But may I cure that habit, look up and outwards
  And may my feet follow my wider glance
First no doubt to stumble, then to walk with the others
  And in the end – with time and luck – to dance.

iv

September has come and I wake
  And I think with joy how whatever, now or in future,
    the system
Nothing whatever can take
  The people away, there will always be people
For friends or for lovers though perhaps
  The conditions of love will be changed and its vices
    diminished
And affection not lapse
  To narrow possessiveness, jealousy founded on vanity.
September has come, it is *hers*
  Whose vitality leaps in the autumn,
Whose nature prefers
  Trees without leaves and a fire in the fire-place;
So I give her this month and the next
  Though the whole of my year should be hers who has
    rendered already
So many of its days intolerable or perplexed
  But so many more so happy;
Who has left a scent on my life and left my walls
  Dancing over and over with her shadow,
Whose hair is twined in all my waterfalls
  And all of London littered with remembered kisses.
So I am glad
  That life contains her with her moods and moments
More shifting and more transient than I had
  Yet thought of as being integral to beauty;
Whose mind is like the wind on a sea of wheat,
  Whose eyes are candour,
And assurance in her feet

Like a homing pigeon never by doubt diverted.
To whom I send my thanks
    That the air has become shot silk, the streets are music,
And that the ranks
    Of men are ranks of men, no more of cyphers.
So that if now alone
    I must pursue this life, it will not be only
A drag from numbered stone to numbered stone
    But a ladder of angels, river turning tidal.
Off-hand, at times hysterical, abrupt,
    You are one I always shall remember,
Whom cant can never corrupt
    Nor argument disinherit.
Frivolous, always in a hurry, forgetting the address,
    Frowning too often, taking enormous notice
Of hats and backchat – how could I assess
    The thing that makes you different?
You whom I remember glad or tired,
    Smiling in drink or scintillating anger,
Inopportunely desired
    On boats, on trains, on roads when walking.
Sometimes untidy, often elegant,
    So easily hurt, so readily responsive,
To whom a trifle could be an irritant
    Or could be balm and manna.
Whose words would tumble over each other and pelt
    From pure excitement,
Whose fingers curl and melt
    When you were friendly.
I shall remember you in bed with bright
    Eyes or in a café stirring coffee
Abstractedly and on your plate the white
    Smoking stub your lips had touched with crimson.

And I shall remember how your words could hurt
    Because they were so honest
And even your lies were able to assert
    Integrity of purpose.
And it is on the strength of knowing you
    I reckon generous feeling more important
Than the mere deliberating what to do
    When neither the pros nor cons affect the pulses.
And though I have suffered from your special strength
    Who never flatter for points nor fake responses,
I should be proud if I could evolve at length
    An equal thrust and pattern.

V

To-day was a beautiful day, the sky was a brilliant
  Blue for the first time for weeks and weeks
But posters flapping on the railings tell the fluttered
  World that Hitler speaks, that Hitler speaks
And we cannot take it in and we go to our daily
  Jobs to the dull refrain of the caption 'War'
Buzzing around us as from hidden insects
  And we think 'This must be wrong, it has happened
    before,
Just like this before, we must be dreaming;
  It was long ago these flies
Buzzed like this, so why are they still bombarding
  The ears if not the eyes?'
And we laugh it off and go round town in the evening
  And this, we say, is on me;
Something out of the usual, a Pimm's Number One, a
    Picon –
  But did you see
The latest? You mean whether Cobb has bust the record
  Or do you mean the Australians have lost their last by
    ten
Wickets or do you mean that the autumn fashions –
  No, we don't mean anything like that again.
No, what we mean is Hodza, Henlein, Hitler,
  The Maginot Line,
The heavy panic that cramps the lungs and presses
  The collar down the spine.
And when we go out into Piccadilly Circus
  They are selling and buying the late
Special editions snatched and read abruptly

Beneath the electric signs as crude as Fate.
And the individual, powerless, has to exert the
    Powers of will and choice
And choose between enormous evils, either
    Of which depends on somebody else's voice.
The cylinders are racing in the presses,
    The mines are laid,
The ribbon plumbs the fallen fathoms of Wall Street,
    And you and I are afraid.
To-day they were building in Oxford Street, the mortar
    Pleasant to smell,
But now it seems futility, imbecility,
    To be building shops when nobody can tell
What will happen next. What will happen
    We ask and waste the question on the air;
Nelson is stone and Johnnie Walker moves his
    Legs like a cretin over Trafalgar Square.
And in the Corner House the carpet-sweepers
    Advance between the tables after crumbs
Inexorably, like a tank battalion
    In answer to the drums.
In Tottenham Court Road the tarts and negroes
    Loiter beneath the lights
And the breeze gets colder as on so many other
    September nights.
A smell of French bread in Charlotte Street, a rustle
    Of leaves in Regent's Park
And suddenly from the Zoo I hear a sea-lion
    Confidently bark.
And so to my flat with the trees outside the window
    And the dahlia shapes of the lights on Primrose Hill
Whose summit once was used for a gun emplacement
    And very likely will

Be used that way again. The bloody frontier
      Converges on our beds
Like jungle beaters closing in on their destined
      Trophy of pelts and heads.
And at this hour of the day it is no good saying
      'Take away this cup';
Having helped to fill it ourselves it is only logic
      That now we should drink it up.
Nor can we hide our heads in the sands, the sands have
      Filtered away;
Nothing remains but rock at this hour, this zero
      Hour of the day.
Or that is how it seems to me as I listen
      To a hooter call at six
And then a woodpigeon calls and stops but the wind
            continues
      Playing its dirge in the trees, playing its tricks.
And now the dairy cart comes clopping slowly –
      Milk at the doors –
And factory workers are on their way to factories
      And charwomen to chores.
And I notice feathers sprouting from the rotted
      Silk of my black
Double eiderdown which was a wedding
      Present eight years back.
And the linen which I lie on came from Ireland
      In the easy days
When all I thought of was affection and comfort,
      Petting and praise.
And now the woodpigeon starts again denying
      The values of the town
And a car having crossed the hill accelerates, changes
      Up, having just changed down.

And a train begins to chug and I wonder what the
    morning
  Paper will say,
And decide to go quickly to sleep for the morning already
  Is with us, the day is to-day.

And I remember Spain
    At Easter ripe as an egg for revolt and ruin
Though for a tripper the rain
    Was worse than the surly or the worried or the haunted
      faces
With writings on the walls –
    Hammer and sickle, Boicot, Viva, Muerra;
With café-au-lait brimming the waterfalls,
    With sherry, shellfish, omelettes.
With fretted stone the Moor
    Had chiselled for effects of sun and shadow;
With shadows of the poor,
    The begging cripples and the children begging.
The churches full of saints
    Tortured on racks of marble –
The old complaints
    Covered with gilt and dimly lit with candles.
With powerful or banal
    Monuments of riches or repression
And the Escorial
    Cold for ever within like the heart of Philip.
With ranks of dominoes
    Deployed on café tables the whole of Sunday;
With cabarets that call the tourist, shows
    Of thighs and eyes and nipples.
With slovenly soldiers, nuns,
    And peeling posters from the last elections
Promising bread or guns
    Or an amnesty or another
Order or else the old

Glory veneered and varnished
As if veneer could hold
    The rotten guts and crumbled bones together.
And a vulture hung in air
    Below the cliffs of Ronda and below him
His hook-winged shadow wavered like despair
    Across the chequered vineyards.
And the boot-blacks in Madrid
    Kept us half an hour with polish and pincers
And all we did
    In that city was drink and think and loiter.
And in the Prado half-
    wit princes looked from the canvas they had paid for
(Goya had the laugh –
    But can what is corrupt be cured by laughter?)
And the day at Aranjuez
    When the sun came out for once on the yellow river
With Valdepeñas burdening the breath
    We slept a royal sleep in the royal gardens;
And at Toledo walked
    Around the ramparts where they throw the garbage
And glibly talked
    Of how the Spaniards lack all sense of business.
And Avila was cold
    And Segovia was picturesque and smelly
And a goat on the road seemed old
    As the rocks or the Roman arches.
And Easter was wet and full
    In Seville and in the ring on Easter Sunday
A clumsy bull and then a clumsy bull
    Nodding his banderillas died of boredom.
And the standard of living was low
    But that, we thought to ourselves, was not our business;

All that the tripper wants is the *status quo*
  Cut and dried for trippers.
And we thought the papers a lark
  With their party politics and blank invective;
And we thought the dark
  Women who dyed their hair should have it dyed more
    often.
And we sat in trains all night
  With the windows shut among civil guards and peasants
And tried to play piquet by a tiny light
  And tried to sleep bolt upright;
And cursed the Spanish rain
  And cursed their cigarettes which came to pieces
And caught heavy colds in Cordova and in vain
  Waited for the right light for taking photos.
And we met a Cambridge don who said with an air
  'There's going to be trouble shortly in this country,'
And ordered anis, pudgy and debonair,
  Glad to show off his mastery of the language.
But only an inch behind
  This map of olive and ilex, this painted hoarding,
Careless of visitors the people's mind
  Was tunnelling like a mole to day and danger.
And the day before we left
  We saw the mob in flower at Algeciras
Outside a toothless door, a church bereft
  Of its images and its aura.
And at La Linea while
  The night put miles between us and Gibraltar
We heard the blood-lust of a drunkard pile
  His heaven high with curses;
And next day took the boat
  For home, forgetting Spain, not realising

20

That Spain would soon denote
    Our grief, our aspirations;
Not knowing that our blunt
    Ideals would find their whetstone, that our spirit
Would find its frontier on the Spanish front,
    Its body in a rag-tag army.

vii

Conferences, adjournments, ultimatums,
  Flights in the air, castles in the air,
The autopsy of treaties, dynamite under the bridges,
  The end of *laissez-faire*.
After the warm days the rain comes pimpling
  The paving stones with white
And with the rain the national conscience, creeping,
  Seeping through the night.
And in the sodden park on Sunday protest
  Meetings assemble not, as so often, now
Merely to advertise some patent panacea
  But simply to avow
The need to hold the ditch; a bare avowal
  That may perhaps imply
Death at the doors in a week but perhaps in the long run
  Exposure of the lie.
Think of a number, double it, treble it, square it,
  And sponge it out
And repeat *ad lib.* and mark the slate with crosses;
  There is no time to doubt
If the puzzle really has an answer. Hitler yells on the
    wireless,
  The night is damp and still
And I hear dull blows on wood outside my window;
  They are cutting down the trees on Primrose Hill.
The wood is white like the roast flesh of chicken,
  Each tree falling like a closing fan;
No more looking at the view from seats beneath the
    branches,
  Everything is going to plan;

They want the crest of this hill for anti-aircraft,
  The guns will take the view
And searchlights probe the heavens for bacilli
  With narrow wands of blue.
And the rain came on as I watched the territorials
  Sawing and chopping and pulling on ropes like a team
In a village tug-of-war; and I found my dog had vanished
  And thought 'This is the end of the old régime,'
But found the police had got her at St. John's Wood
    station
  And fetched her in the rain and went for a cup
Of coffee to an all-night shelter and heard a taxi-driver
  Say 'It turns me up
When I see these soldiers in lorries' – rumble of tumbrils
  Drums in the trees
Breaking the eardrums of the ravished dryads –
  It turns me up; a coffee, please.
And as I go out I see a windscreen-wiper
  In an empty car
Wiping away like mad and I feel astounded
  That things have gone so far.
And I come back here to my flat and wonder whether
  From now on I need take
The trouble to go out choosing stuff for curtains
  As I don't know anyone to make
Curtains quickly. Rather one should quickly
  Stop the cracks for gas or dig a trench
And take one's paltry measures against the coming
  Of the unknown Uebermensch.
But one – meaning I – is bored, am bored, the issue
  Involving principle but bound in fact
To squander principle in panic and self-deception –
  Accessories after the act,

So that all we foresee is rivers in spate sprouting
  With drowning hands
And men like dead frogs floating till the rivers
  Lose themselves in the sands.
And we who have been brought up to think of 'Gallant
    Belgium'
  As so much blague
Are now preparing again to essay good through evil
  For the sake of Prague;
And must, we suppose, become uncritical, vindictive,
  And must, in order to beat
The enemy, model ourselves upon the enemy,
  A howling radio for our paraclete.
The night continues wet, the axe keeps falling,
  The hill grows bald and bleak
No longer one of the sights of London but maybe
  We shall have fireworks here by this day week.

viii

Sun shines easy, sun shines gay
  On bug-house, warehouse, brewery, market,
On the chocolate factory and the B.S.A.,
  On the Greek town hall and Josiah Mason;
On the Mitchells and Butlers Tudor pubs,
  On the white police and the one-way traffic
And glances off the chromium hubs
  And the metal studs in the sleek macadam.
Eight years back about this time
  I came to live in this hazy city
To work in a building caked with grime
  Teaching the classics to Midland students;
Virgil, Livy, the usual round,
  Principal parts and the lost digamma;
And to hear the prison-like lecture room resound
  To Homer in a Dudley accent.
But Life was comfortable, life was fine
  With two in a bed and patchwork cushions
And checks and tassels on the washing-line,
  A gramophone, a cat, and the smell of jasmine.
The steaks were tender, the films were fun,
  The walls were striped like a Russian ballet,
There were lots of things undone
  But nobody cared, for the days were early.
Nobody niggled, nobody cared,
  The soul was deaf to the mounting debit,
The soul was unprepared
  But the firelight danced on the ply-wood ceiling.
We drove round Shropshire in a bijou car –
  Bewdley, Cleobury Mortimer, Ludlow –

And the map of England was a toy bazaar
   And the telephone wires were idle music.
And sun shone easy, sun shone hard
   On quickly dropping pear-tree blossom
And pigeons courting in the cobbled yard
   With flashing necks and notes of thunder.
We slept in linen, we cooked with wine,
   We paid in cash and took no notice
Of how the train ran down the line
   Into the sun against the signal.
We lived in Birmingham through the slump –
   Line your boots with a piece of paper –
Sunlight dancing on the rubbish dump,
   On the queues of men and the hungry chimneys.
And the next election came –
   Labour defeats in Erdington and Aston;
And life went on – for us went on the same;
   Who were we to count the losses?
Some went back to work and the void
   Took on shape while others climbing
The uphill nights of the unemployed
   Woke in the morning to factory hooters.
Little on the plate and nothing in the post;
   Queue in the rain or try the public
Library where the eye may coast
   Columns of print for a hopeful harbour.
But roads ran easy, roads ran gay
   Clear of the city and we together
Could put on tweeds for a getaway
   South or west to Clee or the Cotswolds;
Forty to the gallon; into the green
   Fields in the past of English history;
Flies in the bonnet and dust on the screen

And no look back to the burning city.
That was then and now is now,
   Here again on a passing visit,
Passing through but how
   Memory blocks the passage.
Just as in Nineteen-Thirty-One
   Sun shines easy but I no longer
Docket a place in the sun –
   No wife, no ivory tower, no funk-hole.
The night grows purple, the crisis hangs
   Over the roofs like a Persian army
And all of Xenophon's parasangs
   Would take us only an inch from danger.
Black-out practice and A.R.P.,
   Newsboys driving a roaring business,
The flapping paper snatched to see
   If anything has, or has not, happened.
And I go to the Birmingham Hippodrome
   Packed to the roof and primed for laughter
And beautifully at home
   With the ukulele and the comic chestnuts;
'As pals we meet, as pals we part' –
   Embonpoint and a new tiara;
The comedian spilling the apple-cart
   Of doubles entendres and doggerel verses
And the next day begins
   Again with alarm and anxious
Listening to bulletins
   From distant, measured voices
Arguing for peace
   While the zero hour approaches,
While the eagles gather and the petrol and oil and grease
   Have all been applied and the vultures back the eagles.

But once again
   The crisis is put off and things look better
And we feel negotiation is not vain –
   Save my skin and damn my conscience.
And negotiation wins,
   If you can call it winning,
And here we are – just as before – safe in our skins;
   Glory to God for Munich.
And stocks go up and wrecks
   Are salved and politicians' reputations
Go up like Jack-on-the-Beanstalk; only the Czechs
   Go down and without fighting.

ix

Now we are back to normal, now the mind is
  Back to the even tenor of the usual day
Skidding no longer across the uneasy camber
  Of the nightmare way.
We are safe though others have crashed the railings
  Over the river ravine; their wheel-tracks carve the bank
But after the event all we can do is argue
  And count the widening ripples where they sank.
October comes with rain whipping around the ankles
  In waves of white at night
And filling the raw clay trenches (the parks of London
  Are a nasty sight).
In a week I return to work, lecturing, coaching,
  As impresario of the Ancient Greeks
Who wore the chiton and lived on fish and olives
  And talked philosophy or smut in cliques;
Who believed in youth and did not gloze the unpleasant
  Consequences of age;
What is life, one said, or what is pleasant
  Once you have turned the page
Of love? The days grow worse, the dice are loaded
  Against the living man who pays in tears for breath;
Never to be born was the best, call no man happy
  This side death.
Conscious – long before Engels – of necessity
  And therein free
They plotted out their life with truism and humour
  Between the jealous heaven and the callous sea.
And Pindar sang the garland of wild olive
  And Alcibiades lived from hand to mouth

Double-crossing Athens, Persia, Sparta,
    And many died in the city of plague, and many of
        drouth
In Sicilian quarries, and many by the spear and arrow
    And many more who told their lies too late
Caught in the eternal factions and reactions
    Of the city-state.
And free speech shivered on the pikes of Macedonia
    And later on the swords of Rome
And Athens became a mere university city
    And the goddess born of the foam
Became the kept hetaera, heroine of Menander,
    And the philosopher narrowed his focus, confined
His efforts to putting his own soul in order
    And keeping a quiet mind.
And for a thousand years they went on talking,
    Making such apt remarks,
A race no longer of heroes but of professors
    And crooked business men and secretaries and clerks;
Who turned out dapper little elegiac verses
    On the ironies of fate, the transience of all
Affections, carefully shunning an over-statement
    But working the dying fall.
The Glory that was Greece: put it in a syllabus, grade it
    Page by page
To train the mind or even to point a moral
    For the present age:
Models of logic and lucidity, dignity, sanity,
    The golden mean between opposing ills
Though there were exceptions of course but only
        exceptions –
    The bloody Bacchanals on the Thracian hills.
So the humanist in his room with Jacobean panels

Chewing his pipe and looking on a lazy quad
Chops the Ancient World to turn a sermon
    To the greater glory of God.
But I can do nothing so useful or so simple;
    These dead are dead
And when I should remember the paragons of Hellas
    I think instead
Of the crooks, the adventurers, the opportunists,
    The careless athletes and the fancy boys,
The hair-splitters, the pedants, the hard-boiled sceptics
    And the Agora and the noise
Of the demagogues and the quacks; and the women
        pouring
    Libations over graves
And the trimmers at Delphi and the dummies at Sparta
        and lastly
    I think of the slaves.
And how one can imagine oneself among them
    I do not know;
It was all so unimaginably different
    And all so long ago.

X

And so return to work – the M.A. gown,
  Alphas and Betas, central heating, floor-polish,
Demosthenes on the Crown
  And Oedipus at Colonus.
And I think of the beginnings of other terms
  Coming across the sea to unknown England
And memory reaffirms
  That alarm and exhilaration of arrival:
White wooden boxes, clatter of boots, a smell
  Of changing-rooms – Lifebuoy soap and muddy
    flannels –
And over all a bell
  Dragooning us to dormitory or classroom,
Ringing with a tongue of frost across the bare
  Benches and desks escutcheoned with initials;
We sat on the hot pipes by the wall, aware
  Of the cold in our bones and the noise and the bell
    impending.
A fishtail gas-flare in the dark latrine;
  Chalk and ink and rows of pegs and lockers;
The War was on – maize and margarine
  And lessons on the map of Flanders.
But we had our toys – our electric torches, our glass
  Dogs and cats, and plasticine and conkers,
And we had our games, we learned to dribble and pass
  In jerseys striped like tigers.
And we had our makebelieve, we had our mock
  Freedom in walks by twos and threes on Sunday,
We dug out fossils from the yellow rock
  Or drank the Dorset distance.

And we had our little tiptoe minds, alert
    To jump for facts and fancies and statistics
And our little jokes of Billy Bunter dirt
    And a heap of home-made dogma.
The Abbey chimes varnished the yellow street,
    The water from the taps in the bath was yellow,
The trees were full of owls, the sweets were sweet
    And life an expanding ladder.
And reading romances we longed to be grown up,
    To shoot from the hip and marry lovely ladies
And smoke cigars and live on claret cup
    And lie in bed in the morning;
Taking it for granted that things would still
    Get better and bigger and better and bigger and better,
That the road across the hill
    Led to the Garden of Eden;
Everything to expect and nothing to deplore,
    Cushy days beyond the dumb horizon
And nothing to doubt about, to linger for
    In the halfway house of childhood.
And certainly we did not linger, we went on
    Growing and growing, gluttons for the future,
And four foot six was gone
    And we found it was time to be leaving
To be changing school, sandstone changed for chalk
    And ammonites for the flinty husks of sponges,
Another lingo to talk
    And jerseys in other colours.
And still the acquiring of unrelated facts,
    A string of military dates for history,
And the Gospels and the Acts
    And logarithms and Greek and the Essays of Elia;
And still the exhilarating rhythm of free

Movement swimming or serving at tennis,
The fives-courts' tattling repartee
    Or rain on the sweating body.
But life began to narrow to what was done –
    The dominant gerundive –
And Number Two must mimic Number One
    In bearing, swearing, attitude and accent.
And so we jettisoned all
    Our childish fantasies and anarchism;
The weak must go to the wall
    But strength implies the system;
You must lose your soul to be strong, you cannot stand
    Alone on your own legs or your own ideas;
The order of the day is complete conformity and
    An automatic complacence.
Such was the order of the day; only at times
    The Fool among the yes-men flashed his motley
To prick their pseudo-reason with his rhymes
    And drop his grain of salt on court behaviour.
And sometimes a whisper in books
    Would challenge the code, or a censored memory
        sometimes,
Sometimes the explosion of rooks,
    Sometimes the mere batter of light on the senses.
And the critic jailed in the mind would peep through the
        grate
    And husky from long silence, murmur gently
That there is something rotten in the state
    Of Denmark but the state is not the whole of Denmark;
And a spade is still a spade
    And the difference is not final between a tailored
Suit and a ready-made
    And knowledge is not – necessarily – wisdom;

And a cultured accent alone will not provide
    A season ticket to the Vita Nuova;
And there are many better men outside
    Than ever answered roll-call.
But the critic did not win, has not won yet
    Though always reminding us of points forgotten;
We hasten to forget
    As much as he remembers.
And school was what they always said it was,
    An apprenticeship to life, an initiation,
And all the better because
    The initiates were blindfold;
The reflex action of a dog or sheep
    Being enough for normal avocations
And life rotating in an office sleep
    As long as things are normal.
Which it was assumed that they would always be;
    On that assumption terms began and ended;
And now, in Nineteen-Thirty-Eight A.D.,
    Term is again beginning.

xi

But work is alien; what do I care for the Master
   Of those who know, of those who know too much?
I am too harassed by my familiar devils,
   By those I cannot see, by those I may not touch;
Knowing perfectly well in the mind, on paper,
   How wasteful and absurd
Are personal fixations but yet the pulse keeps thrumming
   And her voice is faintly heard
Through walls and walls of indifference and abstraction
   And across the London roofs
And every so often calls up hopes from nowhere,
   A distant clatter of hoofs,
And my common sense denies she is returning
   And says, if she does return, she will not stay;
And my pride, in the name of reason, tells me to cut my
      losses
   And call it a day.
Which, if I had the cowardice of my convictions,
   I certainly should do
But doubt still finds a loophole
   To gamble on another rendezvous.
And I try to feel her in fancy but the fancy
   Dissolves in curls of mist
And I try to summarise her but how can hungry
   Love be a proper analyst?
For suddenly I hate her and would murder
   Her memory if I could
And then of a sudden I see her sleeping gently
   Inaccessible in a sleeping wood
But thorns and thorns around her

And the cries of night
And I have no knife or axe to hack my passage
    Back to the lost delight.
And then I think of the others and jealousy riots
    In impossible schemes
To kill them with all the machinery of fact and with all the
    Tortures of dreams.
But yet, my dear, if only for my own distraction,
    I have to try to assess
Your beauty of body, your paradoxes of spirit,
    Even your taste in dress.
Whose emotions are an intricate dialectic,
    Whose eagerness to live
A many-sided life might be deplored as fickle,
    Unpractical, or merely inquisitive.
A superficial comment; for your instinct
    Sanctions all you do,
Who know that truth is nothing in abstraction,
    That action makes both wish and principle come true;
Whose changes have the logic of a prism,
    Whose moods create,
Who never linger haggling on the threshold,
    To weigh the pros and cons until it is too late.
At times intractable, virulent, hypercritical,
    With a bitter tongue;
Over-shy at times, morose, defeatist,
    At times a token that the world is young;
Given to over-statement, careless of caution,
    Quick to sound the chimes
Of delicate intuition, at times malicious
    And generous at times.
Whose kaleidoscopic ways are all authentic,
    Whose truth is not of a statement but of a dance

So that even when you deceive your deceits are merely
  Technical and of no significance.
And so, when I think of you, I have to meet you
  In thought on your own ground;
To apply to you my algebraic canons
  Would merely be unsound;
And, having granted this, I cannot balance
  My hopes or fears of you in pros and cons;
It has been proved that Achilles cannot catch the Tortoise,
  It has been proved that men are automatons,
Everything wrong has been proved. I will not bother
  Any more with proof;
I see the future glinting with your presence
  Like moon on a slate roof,
And my spirits rise again. It is October,
  The year-god dying on the destined pyre
With all the colours of a scrambled sunset
  And all the funeral elegance of fire
In the grey world to lie cocooned but shaping
  His gradual return;
No one can stop the cycle;
  The grate is full of ash but fire will always burn.
Therefore, listening to the taxis
  (In which you never come) so regularly pass,
I wait content, banking on the spring and watching
  The dead leaves canter over the dowdy grass.

xii

These days are misty, insulated, mute
    Like a faded tapestry and the soft pedal
Is down and the yellow leaves are falling down
    And we hardly have the heart to meddle
Any more with personal ethics or public calls;
    People have not recovered from the crisis,
Their faces are far away, the tone of the words
    Belies their thesis.
For they say that now it is time unequivocally to act,
    To let the pawns be taken,
That criticism, a virtue previously,
    Now can only weaken
And that when we go to Rome
    We must do as the Romans do, cry out together
For bread and circuses; put on your togas now
    For this is Roman weather.
Circuses of death and from the topmost tiers
    A cataract of goggling, roaring faces;
On the arena sand
    Those who are about to die try out their paces.
Now it is night, a cold mist creeps, the night
    Is still and damp and lonely;
Sitting by the fire it is hard to realise
    That the legions wait at the gates and that there is only
A little time for rest though not by rights for rest,
    Rather for whetting the will, for calculating
A compromise between necessity and wish,
    Apprenticed late to learn the trade of hating.
Remember the sergeant barking at bayonet practice
    When you were small;

To kill a dummy you must act a dummy
  Or you cut no ice at all.
Now it is morning again, the 25th of October,
  In a white fog the cars have yellow lights;
The chill creeps up the wrists, the sun is sallow,
  The silent hours grow down like stalactites.
And reading Plato talking about his Forms
  To damn the artist touting round his mirror,
I am glad that I have been left the third best bed
  And live in a world of error.
His world of capital initials, of transcendent
  Ideas is too bleak;
For me there remain to all intents and purposes
  Seven days in the week
And no one Tuesday is another and you destroy it
  If you subtract the difference and relate
It merely to the Form of Tuesday. This is Tuesday
  The 25th of October, 1938.
Aristotle was better who watched the insect breed,
  The natural world develop,
Stressing the function, scrapping the Form in Itself,
  Taking the horse from the shelf and letting it gallop.
Education gives us too many labels
  And clichés, cuts too many Gordian knots;
Trains us to keep the roads nor reconnoitre
  Any of the beauty-spots or danger-spots.
Not that I would rather be a peasant; the Happy Peasant
  Like the Noble Savage is a myth;
I do not envy the self-possession of an elm-tree
  Nor the aplomb of a granite monolith.
All that I would like to be is human, having a share
  In a civilised, articulate and well-adjusted
Community where the mind is given its due

But the body is not distrusted.
As it is, the so-called humane studies
    May lead to cushy jobs
But leave the men who land them spiritually bankrupt
    Intellectual snobs.
Not but what I am glad to have my comforts,
    Better authentic mammon than a bogus god;
If it were not for Lit.Hum. I might be climbing
    A ladder with a hod.
And seven hundred a year
    Will pay the rent and the gas and the 'phone and the
        grocer;
(The Emperor takes his seat beneath the awning,
    Those who are about to die . . .) Come, pull the curtains
        closer.

xiii

Which things being so, as we said when we studied
    The classics, I ought to be glad
That I studied the classics at Marlborough and Merton,
    Not everyone here having had
The privilege of learning a language
    That is incontrovertibly dead,
And of carting a toy-box of hall-marked marmoreal
      phrases
    Around in his head.
We wrote compositions in Greek which they said was a
      lesson
    In logic and good for the brain;
We marched, counter-marched to the field-marshal's blue-
      pencil baton,
    We dressed by the right and we wrote out the sentence
      again.
We learned that a gentleman never misplaces his accents,
    That nobody knows how to speak, much less how to
      write
English who has not hob-nobbed with the great-
      grandparents of English,
    That the boy on the Modern Side is merely a parasite
But the classical student is bred to the purple, his training
      in syntax
    Is also a training in thought
And even in morals; if called to the bar or the barracks
    He always will do what he ought.
And knowledge, besides, should be prized for the sake of
      knowledge:
    Oxford crowded the mantelpiece with gods –

Scaliger, Heinsius, Dindorf, Bentley and Wilamowitz –
   As we learned our genuflexions for Honour Mods.
And then they taught us philosophy, logic and
      metaphysics,
   The Negative Judgment and the Ding an Sich,
And every single thinker was powerful as Napoleon
   And crafty as Metternich.
And it really was very attractive to be able to talk about
      tables
   And to ask if the table *is*,
And to draw the cork out of an old conundrum
   And watch the paradoxes fizz.
And it made one confident to think that nothing
   Really was what it seemed under the sun,
That the actual was not real and the real was not with us
   And all that mattered was the One.
And they said 'The man in the street is so naïve, he never
   Can see the wood for the trees;
He thinks he knows he sees a thing but cannot
   Tell you how he knows the thing he thinks he sees.'
And oh how much I liked the Concrete Universal,
   I never thought that I should
Be telling them vice-versa
   That they can't see the trees for the wood.
But certainly it was fun while it lasted
   And I got my honours degree
And was stamped as a person of intelligence and culture
   For ever wherever two or three
Persons of intelligence and culture
   Are gathered together in talk
Writing definitions on invisible blackboards
   In non-existent chalk.
But such sacramental occasions

Are nowadays comparatively rare;
There is always a wife or a boss or a dun or a client
   Disturbing the air.
Barbarians always, life in the particular always,
   Dozens of men in the street,
And the perennial if unimportant problem
   Of getting enough to eat.
So blow the bugles over the metaphysicians,
   Let the pure mind return to the Pure Mind;
I must be content to remain in the world of Appearance
   And sit on the mere appearance of a behind.
But in case you should think my education was wasted
   I hasten to explain
That having once been to the University of Oxford
   You can never really again
Believe anything that anyone says and that of course is an
     asset
   In a world like ours;
Why bother to water a garden
   That is planted with paper flowers?
O the Freedom of the Press, the Late Night Final,
   To-morrow's pulp;
One should not gulp one's port but as it isn't
   Port, I'll gulp it if I want to gulp
But probably I'll just enjoy the colour
   And pour it down the sink
For I don't call advertisement a statement
   Or any quack medicine a drink.
Good-bye now, Plato and Hegel,
   The shop is closing down;
They don't want any philosopher-kings in England,
   There ain't no universals in this man's town.

xiv

The next day I drove by night
  Among red and amber and green, spears and candles,
Corkscrews and slivers of reflected light
  In the mirror of the rainy asphalt
Along the North Circular and the Great West roads
  Running the gauntlet of impoverished fancy
Where housewives bolster up their jerry-built abodes
  With *amour propre* and the habit of Hire Purchase.
The wheels whished in the wet, the flashy strings
  Of neon lights unravelled, the windscreen-wiper
Kept at its job like a tiger in a cage or a cricket that sings
  All night through for nothing.
Factory, a site for a factory, rubbish dumps,
  Bungalows in lath and plaster, in brick, in concrete,
And shining semi-circles of petrol pumps
  Like intransigent gangs of idols.
And the road swings round my head like a lassoo
  Looping wider and wider tracts of darkness
And the country succeeds the town and the country too
  Is damp and dark and evil.
And coming over the Chilterns the dead leaves leap
  Charging the windscreen like a barrage of angry
Birds as I take the steep
  Plunge to Henley or Hades.
And at the curves of the road the telephone wires
  Shine like strands of silk and the hedge solicits
My irresponsible tyres
  To an accident, to a bed in the wet grasses.
And in quiet crooked streets only the village pub
  Spills a golden puddle

Over the pavement and trees bend down and rub
   Unopened dormer windows with their knuckles.
Nettlebed, Shillingford, Dorchester – each unrolls
   The road to Oxford; *Qu'allais-je faire* to-morrow
Driving voters to the polls
   In that home of lost illusions?
And what am I doing it for?
   Mainly for fun, partly for a half-believed-in
Principle, a core
   Of fact in a pulp of verbiage,
Remembering that this crude and so-called obsolete
   Top-heavy tedious parliamentary system
Is our only ready weapon to defeat
   The legions' eagles and the lictors' axes;
And remembering that those who by their habit hate
   Politics can no longer keep their private
Values unless they open the public gate
   To a better political system.
That Rome was not built in a day is no excuse
   For *laissez-faire*, for bowing to the odds against us;
What is the use
   Of asking what is the use of one brick only?
The perfectionist stands for ever in a fog
   Waiting for the fog to clear; better to be vulgar
And use your legs and leave a blank for Hogg
   And put a cross for Lindsay.
There are only too many who say 'What difference does it make
   One way or the other?
To turn the stream of history will take
   More than a by-election.'
So Thursday came and Oxford went to the polls
   And made its coward vote and the streets resounded

To the triumphant cheers of the lost souls –
  The profiteers, the dunderheads, the smarties.
And I drove back to London in the dark of the morning,
      the trees
  Standing out in the headlights cut from cardboard;
Wondering which disease
  Is worse – the Status Quo or the Mere Utopia.
For from now on
  Each occasion must be used, however trivial,
To rally the ranks of those whose chance will soon be gone
  For even guerrilla warfare.
The nicest people in England have always been the least
  Apt to solidarity or alignment
But all of them must now align against the beast
  That prowls at every door and barks in every headline.
Dawn and London and daylight and last the sun:
  I stop the car and take the yellow placard
Off the bonnet; that little job is done
  Though without success or glory.
The plane-tree leaves come sidling down
  (Catch my guineas, catch my guineas)
And the sun caresses Camden Town,
  The barrows of oranges and apples.

XV

Shelley and jazz and lieder and love and hymn-tunes
  And day returns too soon;
We'll get drunk among the roses
  In the valley of the moon.
Give me an aphrodisiac, give me lotus,
  Give me the same again;
Make all the erotic poets of Rome and Ionia
  And Florence and Provence and Spain
Pay a tithe of their sugar to my potion
  And ferment my days
With the twang of Hawaii and the boom of the Congo;
  Let the old Muse loosen her stays
Or give me a new Muse with stockings and suspenders
  And a smile like a cat,
With false eyelashes and finger-nails of carmine
  And dressed by Schiaparelli, with a pill-box hat.
Let the aces run riot round Brooklands,
  Let the tape-machines go drunk,
Turn on the purple spotlight, pull out the Vox Humana,
  Dig up somebody's body in a cloakroom trunk.
Give us sensations and then again sensations –
  Strip-tease, fireworks, all-in wrestling, gin;
Spend your capital, open your house and pawn your
      padlocks,
  Let the critical sense go out and the Roaring Boys come
      in.
Give me a houri but houris are too easy,
  Give me a nun;
We'll rape the angels off the golden reredos
  Before we're done.

48

Tiger-women and Lesbos, drums and entrails,
    And let the skies rotate,
We'll play roulette with the stars, we'll sit out drinking
    At the Hangman's Gate.
O look who comes here. I cannot see their faces
    Walking in file, slowly in file;
They have no shoes on their feet, the knobs of their ankles
    Catch the moonlight as they pass the stile
And cross the moor among the skeletons of bog-oak
    Following the track from the gallows back to the town;
Each has the end of a rope around his neck. I wonder
    Who let these men come back, who cut them down –
And now they reach the gate and line up opposite
    The neon lights on the medieval wall
And underneath the sky-signs
    Each one takes his cowl and lets it fall
And we see their faces, each the same as the other,
    Men and women, each like a closed door,
But something about their faces is familiar;
    Where have we seen them before?
Was it the murderer on the nursery ceiling
    Or Judas Iscariot in the Field of Blood
Or someone at Gallipoli or in Flanders
    Caught in the end-all mud.
But take no notice of them, out with the ukulele,
    The saxophone and the dice;
They are sure to go away if we take no notice;
    Another round of drinks or make it twice.
That was a good one, tell us another, don't stop talking,
    Cap your stories; if
You haven't any new ones tell the old ones,
    Tell them as often as you like and perhaps those horrible
        stiff

People with blank faces that are yet familiar
    Won't be there when you look again, but don't
Look just yet, just give them time to vanish. I said to
      vanish;
    What do you mean – they won't?
Give us the songs of Harlem or Mitylene –
    Pearls in wine –
There can't be a hell unless there is a heaven
    And a devil would have to be divine
And there can't be such things one way or the other;
    That we know;
You can't step into the same river twice so there can't be
    Ghosts; thank God that rivers always flow.
Sufficient to the moment is the moment;
    Past and future merely don't make sense
And yet I thought I had seen them . . .
    But *how*, if there is only a present tense?
Come on, boys, we aren't afraid of bogies,
    Give us another drink;
This little lady has a fetish,
    She goes to bed in mink.
This little pig went to market –
    Now I think you may look, I think the coast is clear.
Well, why don't you answer?
    I can't answer because they are still there.

XVI

Nightmare leaves fatigue:
  We envy men of action
Who sleep and wake, murder and intrigue
  Without being doubtful, without being haunted.
And I envy the intransigence of my own
  Countrymen who shoot to kill and never
See the victim's face become their own
  Or find his motive sabotage their motives.
So reading the memoirs of Maud Gonne,
  Daughter of an English mother and a soldier father,
I note how a single purpose can be founded on
  A jumble of opposites:
Dublin Castle, the vice-regal ball,
  The embassies of Europe,
Hatred scribbled on a wall,
  Gaols and revolvers.
And I remember, when I was little, the fear
  Bandied among the servants
That Casement would land at the pier
  With a sword and a horde of rebels;
And how we used to expect, at a later date,
  When the wind blew from the west, the noise of
    shooting
Starting in the evening at eight
  In Belfast in the York Street district;
And the voodoo of the Orange bands
  Drawing an iron net through darkest Ulster,
Flailing the limbo lands –
  The linen mills, the long wet grass, the ragged
    hawthorn.

And one read black where the other read white, his hope
    The other man's damnation:
Up the Rebels, To Hell with the Pope,
    And God Save – as you prefer – the King or Ireland.
The land of scholars and saints:
    Scholars and saints my eye, the land of ambush,
Purblind manifestoes, never-ending complaints,
    The born martyr and the gallant ninny;
The grocer drunk with the drum,
    The land-owner shot in his bed, the angry voices
Piercing the broken fanlight in the slum,
    The shawled woman weeping at the garish altar.
Kathaleen ni Houlihan! Why
    Must a country, like a ship or a car, be always female,
Mother or sweetheart? A woman passing by,
    We did but see her passing.
Passing like a patch of sun on the rainy hill
    And yet we love her for ever and hate our neighbour
And each one in his will
    Binds his heirs to continuance of hatred.
Drums on the haycock, drums on the harvest, black
    Drums in the night shaking the windows:
King William is riding his white horse back
    To the Boyne on a banner.
Thousands of banners, thousands of white
    Horses, thousands of Williams
Waving thousands of swords and ready to fight
    Till the blue sea turns to orange.
Such was my country and I thought I was well
    Out of it, educated and domiciled in England,
Though yet her name keeps ringing like a bell
    In an under-water belfry.
Why do we like being Irish? Partly because

It gives us a hold on the sentimental English
As members of a world that never was,
　　Baptised with fairy water;
And partly because Ireland is small enough
　　To be still thought of with a family feeling,
And because the waves are rough
　　That split her from a more commercial culture;
And because one feels that here at least one can
　　Do local work which is not at the world's mercy
And that on this tiny stage with luck a man
　　Might see the end of one particular action.
It is self-deception of course;
　　There is no immunity in this island either;
A cart that is drawn by somebody else's horse
　　And carrying goods to somebody else's market.
The bombs in the turnip sack, the sniper from the roof,
　　Griffith, Connolly, Collins, where have they brought us?
Ourselves alone! Let the round tower stand aloof
　　In a world of bursting mortar!
Let the school-children fumble their sums
　　In a half-dead language;
Let the censor be busy on the books; pull down the
　　　　Georgian slums;
　　Let the games be played in Gaelic.
Let them grow beet-sugar; let them build
　　A factory in every hamlet;
Let them pigeon-hole the souls of the killed
　　Into sheep and goats, patriots and traitors.
And the North, where I was a boy,
　　Is still the North, veneered with the grime of Glasgow,
Thousands of men whom nobody will employ
　　Standing at the corners, coughing.
And the street-children play on the wet

Pavement – hopscotch or marbles;
And each rich family boasts a sagging tennis-net
    On a spongy lawn beside a dripping shrubbery.
The smoking chimneys hint
    At prosperity round the corner
But they make their Ulster linen from foreign lint
    And the money that comes in goes out to make more
        money.
A city built on mud;
    A culture built upon profit;
Free speech nipped in the bud,
    The minority always guilty.
Why should I want to go back
    To you, Ireland, my Ireland?
The blots on the page are so black
    That they cannot be covered with shamrock.
I hate your grandiose airs,
    Your sob-stuff, your laugh and your swagger,
Your assumption that everyone cares
    Who is the king of your castle.
Castles are out of date,
    The tide flows round the children's sandy fancy;
Put up what flag you like, it is too late
    To save your soul with bunting.
Odi atque amo:
    Shall we cut this name on trees with a rusty dagger?
Her mountains are still blue, her rivers flow
    Bubbling over the boulders.
She is both a bore and a bitch;
    Better close the horizon,
Send her no more fantasy, no more longings which
    Are under a fatal tariff.
For common sense is the vogue

And she gives her children neither sense nor money
Who slouch around the world with a gesture and a
    brogue
And a faggot of useless memories.

xvii

From the second floor up, looking north, having breakfast
    I see the November sun at nine o'clock
Gild the fusty brickwork of rows on rows of houses
    Like animals asleep and breathing smoke,
And savouring Well-being
    I light my first cigarette, grow giddy and blink,
Glad of this titillation, this innuendo,
    This make-believe of standing on a brink;
For all our trivial daily acts are altered
    Into heroic or romantic make-believe
Of which we are hardly conscious – Who is it calls me
    When the cold draught picks my sleeve?
Or sneezing in the morning sunlight or smelling the
      bonfire
    Over the webbed lawn and the naked cabbage plot?
Or stepping into a fresh-filled bath with strata
    Of cold water and hot?
We lie in the bath between tiled walls and under
    Ascending scrolls of steam
And feel the ego merge as the pores open
    And we lie in the bath and dream;
And responsibility dies and the thighs are happy
    And the body purrs like a cat
But this lagoon grows cold, we have to leave it, stepping
    On to a check rug on a cork mat.
The luxury life is only to be valued
    By those who are short of money or pressed for time
As the cinema gives the poor their Jacob's ladder
    For Cinderellas to climb.
And Plato was right to define the bodily pleasures

As the pouring water into a hungry sieve
But wrong to ignore the rhythm which the intercrossing
  Coloured waters permanently give.
And Aristotle was right to posit the Alter Ego
  But wrong to make it only a halfway house:
Who could expect – or want – to be spiritually self-
    supporting,
  Eternal self-abuse?
Why not admit that other people are always
  Organic to the self, that a monologue
Is the death of language and that a single lion
  Is less himself, or alive, than a dog and another dog?
Virtue going out of us always; the eyes grow weary
  With vision but it is vision builds the eye;
And in a sense the children kill their parents
  But do the parents die?
And the beloved destroys like fire or water
  But water scours and sculpts and fire refines
And if you are going to read the testaments of cynics,
  You must read between the lines.
A point here and a point there: the current
  Jumps the gaps, the ego cannot live
Without becoming other for the Other
  Has got yourself to give.
And even the sense of taste provides communion
  With God as plant or beast;
The sea in fish, the field in a salad of endive,
  A sacramental feast.
The soul's long searchlight hankers for a body,
  The single body hungers for its kind,
The eye demands the light at the risk of blindness
  And the mind that did not doubt would not be mind
And discontent is eternal. In luxury or business,

In family or sexual love, in purchases or prayers,
Our virtue is invested, the self put out at interest,
    The returns are never enough, the fact compares
So badly with the fancy yet fancy itself is only
    A divination of fact
And if we confine the world to the prophet's tripod
    The subjects of our prophecy contract.
Open the world wide, open the senses,
    Let the soul stretch its blind enormous arms,
There is vision in the fingers only needing waking,
    Ready for light's alarms.
O light, terror of light, hoofs and ruthless
    Wheels of steel and brass
Dragging behind you lacerated captives
    Who also share your triumph as you pass.
Light which is time, belfry of booming sunlight,
    The ropes run up and down,
The whole town shakes with the peal of living people
    Who break and build the town.
Aristotle was right to think of man-in-action
    As the essential and really existent man
And man means men in action; try and confine your
    Self to yourself if you can.
Nothing is self-sufficient, pleasure implies hunger
    But hunger implies hope:
I cannot lie in this bath for ever, clouding
    The cooling water with rose geranium soap.
I cannot drug my life with the present moment;
    The present moment may rape – but all in vain –
The future, for the future remains a virgin
    Who must be tried again.

xviii

In the days that were early the music came easy
    On cradle and coffin, in the corn and the barn,
Songs for the reaping and spinning and only the shepherd
    Then as now was silent beside the tarn:
Cuffs of foam around the beer-brown water,
    Crinkled water and a mackerel sky;
It is all in the day's work – the grey stones and heather
    And the sheep that breed and break their legs and die.
The uplands now as then are fresh but in the valley
    Polluted rivers run – the Lethe and the Styx;
The soil is tired and the profit little and the hunchback
    Bobs on a carthorse round the sodden ricks.
Sing us no more idylls, no more pastorals,
    No more epics of the English earth;
The country is a dwindling annexe to the factory,
    Squalid as an after-birth.
This England is tight and narrow, teeming with unwanted
    Children who are so many, each is alone;
Niobe and her children
    Stand beneath the smokestack turned to stone.
And still the church-bells brag above the empty churches
    And the Union Jack
Thumps the wind above the law-courts and the barracks
    And in the allotments the black
Scarecrow holds a fort of grimy heads of cabbage
    Besieged by grimy birds
Like a hack politician fighting the winged aggressor
    With yesterday's magic coat of ragged words.
Things were different when men felt their programme
    In the bones and pulse, not only in the brain,

Born to a trade, a belief, a set of affections;
    That instinct for belief may sprout again,
There are some who have never lost it
    And some who foster or force it into growth
But most of us lack the right discontent, contented
    Merely to cavil. Spiritual sloth
Creeps like lichen or ivy over the hinges
    Of the doors which never move;
We cannot even remember who is behind them
    Nor even, soon, shall have the chance to prove
If anyone at all is behind them –
    The Sleeping Beauty or the Holy Ghost
Or the greatest happiness of the greatest number;
    All we can do at most
Is press an anxious ear against the keyhole
    To hear the Future breathing; softly tread
In the outer porch beneath the marble volutes –
    Who knows if God, as Nietzsche said, is dead?
There is straw to lay in the streets; call the hunchback,
    The gentleman farmer, the village idiot, the Shropshire
        Lad,
To insulate us if they can with coma
    Before we all go mad.
What shall we pray for, Lord? Whom shall we pray to?
    Shall we give like decadent Athens the benefit of the
        doubt
To the Unknown God or smugly pantheistic
    Assume that God is everywhere round about?
But if we assume such a God, then who the devil
    Are these with empty stomachs or empty smiles?
The blind man's stick goes tapping on the pavement
    For endless glittering miles
Beneath the standard lights; the paralytic winding

His barrel-organ sprays the passers-by
With April music; the many-ribboned hero
　　With half a lung or a leg waits his turn to die.
God forbid an Indian acquiescence,
　　The apotheosis of the status quo;
If everything that happens happens according
　　To the nature and wish of God, then God must go:
Lay your straw in the streets and go about your business
　　An inch at a time, an inch at a time,
We have not even an hour to spend repenting
　　Our sins; the quarters chime
And every minute is its own alarum clock
　　And what we are about to do
Is of vastly more importance
　　Than what we have done or not done hitherto.
It is December now, the trees are naked
　　As the three crosses on the hill;
Through the white fog the face of the orange sun is cryptic
　　Like a lawyer making the year's will.
The year has little to show, will leave a heavy
　　Overdraft to its heir;
Shall we try to meet the deficit or passing
　　By on the other side continue *laissez-faire*?
International betrayals, public murder,
　　The devil quoting scripture, the traitor, the coward, the
　　　　thug
Eating dinner in the name of peace and progress,
　　The doped public sucking a dry dug;
Official recognition of rape, revival of the ghetto
　　And free speech gagged and free
Energy scrapped and dropped like surplus herring
　　Back into the barren sea;
Brains and beauty festering in exile,

The shadow of bars
Falling across each page, each field, each raddled sunset,
    The alien lawn and the pool of nenuphars;
And hordes of homeless poor running the gauntlet
    In hostile city streets of white and violet lamps
Whose flight is without a terminus but better
    Than the repose of concentration camps.
Come over, they said, into Macedonia and help us
    But the chance is gone;
Now we must help ourselves, we can leave the vulture
    To pick the corpses clean in Macedon.
No wonder many would renounce their birthright,
    The responsibility of moral choice,
And sit with a mess of pottage taking orders
    Out of a square box from a mad voice –
Lies on the air endlessly repeated
    Turning the air to fog,
Blanket on blanket of lie, no room to breathe or fidget
    And nobody to jog
Your elbow and say 'Up there the sun is rising;
    Take it on trust, the sun will always shine.'
The sun may shine no doubt but how many people
    Will see it with their eyes in Nineteen-Thirty-Nine?
Yes, the earlier days had their music,
    We have some still to-day,
But the orchestra is due for the bonfire
    If things go on this way.
Still there are still the seeds of energy and choice
    Still alive even if forbidden, hidden,
And while a man has voice
    He may recover music.

xix

The pigeons riddle the London air,
 The shutter slides from the chain-store window,
The frock-coat statue stands in the square
 Caring for no one, caring for no one.
The night-shift men go home to bed,
 The kettle sings and the bacon sizzles;
Some are hungry and some are dead –
 A wistful face in a faded photo.
Under the stairs is a khaki cap;
 That was Dad's, Dad was a plumber –
You hear that dripping tap?
 He'd have had it right in no time.
No time now; Dad is dead,
 He left me five months gone or over;
Tam cari capitis, for such a well-loved head
 What shame in tears, what limit?
It is the child I mean,
 Born prematurely, strangled;
Dad was off the scene,
 He would have made no difference.
The stretchers run from ward to ward,
 The telephone rings in empty houses,
The torn shirt soaks on the scrubbing board,
 O what a busy morning.
Baby Croesus crawls in a pen
 With alphabetical bricks and biscuits;
The doll-dumb file of sandwichmen
 Carry lies from gutter to gutter.
The curate buys his ounce of shag,
 The typist tints her nails with coral,

The housewife with her shopping bag
    Watches the cleaver catch the naked
New Zealand sheep between the legs –
    What price now New Zealand?
The cocker spaniel sits and begs
    With eyes like a waif on the movies.
O what a busy morning,
    Engines start with a roar,
All the wires are buzzing,
    The tape-machines vomit on the floor.
And I feel that my mind once again is open,
    The lady is gone who stood in the way so long,
The hypnosis is over and no one
    Calls encore to the song.
When we are out of love, how were we ever in it?
    Where are the mountains and the mountain skies,
That heady air instinct with
    A strange sincerity which winged our lies?
The peaks have fallen in like dropping pastry:
    Now I could see her come
Around the corner without the pulse responding,
    The flowery orator in the heart is dumb,
His bag of tricks is empty, his over-statements,
    Those rainbow bubbles, have burst:
When we meet, she need not feel embarrassed,
    The cad with the golden tongue has done his worst
And has no orders from me to mix his phrases rich,
    To make the air a carpet
For her to walk on; I only wonder which
    Day, which hour, I found this freedom.
But freedom is not so exciting,
    We prefer to be drawn
In the rush of the stars as they circle –

A traffic that ends with dawn.
Now I am free of the stars
  And the word 'love' makes no sense, this history is
    almost
Ripe for the mind's museum – broken jars
  That once held wine or perfume.
Yet looking at their elegance on the stands
  I feel a certain pride that only lately
(And yet so long ago) I held them in my hands
  While they were full and fragrant.
So on this busy morning I hope, my dear,
  That you are also busy
With another vintage of another year;
  I wish you luck and I thank you for the party –
A good party though at the end my thirst
  Was worse than at the beginning
But never to have drunk no doubt would be the worst;
  Pain, they say, is always twin to pleasure.
Better to have these twins
  Than no children at all, very much better
To act for good and bad than have no sins
  And take no action either.
You were my blizzard who had been my bed.
  But taking the whole series of blight and blossom
I would not choose a simpler crop instead;
  Thank you, my dear – dear against my judgment.

XX

Nelson stands on a black pillar,
  The electric signs go off and on –
Distilleries and life insurance companies –
  The traffic circles, coming and gone,
Past the National Gallery closed and silent
  Where in their frames
Other worlds persist, the passions of the artist
  Caught like frozen flames:
The Primitives distilling from the cruel
  Legend a faith that is almost debonair,
Sebastian calmly waiting the next arrow,
  The crucifixion in the candid air:
And Venice lolling in wealth for ever under glass,
  Pearls in her hair, panther and velvet:
And the rococo picnic on the grass
  With wine and lutes and banter:
And the still life proclaiming with aplomb
  The self-content of bread or fruit or vases
And personality like a silent bomb
  Lurking in the formal portrait.
Here every day the visitors walk slowly
  Rocking along the parquet as if on a ship's deck
Feeling a vague affinity with the pictures
  Yet wary of these waves which gently peck
The side of the boat in passing; they are anxious
  To end the voyage, to land in their own time;
The sea of the past glimmers with white horses,
  A paradigm
Of life's successions, treacheries, recessions;
  The unfounded confidence of the dead affronts

Our own system of values
　　Like airmen doing their stunts
Over our private garden; these arrogant Old Masters
　　Swoop and loop and lance us with a quick
Shadow; we only want to cultivate our garden,
　　Not for us the virtuoso, slick
Tricks of the airy region,
　　For our part our feet are on the ground,
They should not be allowed to fly so low above us,
　　Their premises are unsound
And history has refuted them and yet
　　They cast their shadows on us like aspersions;
Propellers and white horses,
　　Movement, movement, can we never forget
The movements of the past which should be dead?
　　The mind of Socrates still clicks like scissors
And Christ who should lie quiet in the garden
　　Flowered in flame instead.

　　·　　·　　·　　·　　·　　·　　·　　·　　·

A week to Christmas, cards of snow and holly,
　　Gimcracks in the shops,
Wishes and memories wrapped in tissue paper,
　　Trinkets, gadgets and lollipops
And as if through coloured glasses
　　We remember our childhood's thrill
Waking in the morning to the rustling of paper,
　　The eiderdown heaped in a hill
Of wogs and dogs and bears and bricks and apples
　　And the feeling that Christmas Day
Was a coral island in time where we land and eat our lotus
　　But where we can never stay.
There was a star in the East, the magi in their turbans
　　Brought their luxury toys

In homage to a child born to capsize their values
 And wreck their equipoise.
A smell of hay like peace in the dark stable –
 Not peace however but a sword
To cut the Gordian knot of logical self-interest,
 The fool-proof golden cord;
For Christ walked in where no philosopher treads
 But armed with more than folly,
Making the smooth place rough and knocking the heads
 Of Church and State together.
In honour of whom we have taken over the pagan
 Saturnalia for our annual treat
Letting the belly have its say, ignoring
 The spirit while we eat.
And Conscience still goes crying through the desert
 With sackcloth round his loins:
A week to Christmas – hark the herald angels
 Beg for copper coins.

xxi

And when we clear away
   All this debris of day-by-day experience,
What comes out to light, what is there of value
   Lasting from day to day?
I sit in my room in comfort
   Looking at enormous flowers –
Equipment purchased with my working hours,
   A daily mint of perishable petals.
The figures of the dance repeat
   The unending cycle of making and spending money,
Eating our daily bread in order to earn it
   And earning in order to eat.
And is that all the story,
   The mainspring and the plot,
Or merely a mechanism without which not
   Any story could be written?
Sine qua non!
   Sine qua non indeed, we cannot ever
Live by soul alone; the soul without the stomach
   Would find its glory gone.
But the total cause outruns the mere condition,
   There is more to it than that;
Life would be (as it often seems) flat
   If it were merely a matter of not dying.
For each individual then
   Would be fighting a losing battle
But with life as collective creation
   The rout is rallied, the battle begins again.
Only give us the courage of our instinct,
   The will to truth and love's initiative,

Then we could hope to live
   A life beyond the self but self-completing.
And, as the emperor said, What is the use
   Of the minor loyalty – 'Dear city of Cecrops',
Unless we have also the wider franchise, can answer
   'Dear city of Zeus'?
And so when the many regrets
   Trouble us for the many lost affections,
Let us take the wider view before we count them
   Hopelessly bad debts.
For Cecrops has his rights as Zeus has his
   And every tree is a tree of branches
And every wood is a wood of trees growing
   And what has been contributes to what is.
So I am glad to have known them,
   The people or events apparently withdrawn;
The world is round and there is always dawn
   Undeniably somewhere.
'Praised be thou, O Lord, for our brother the sun'
   Said the grey saint, laving his eyes in colour;
Who creates and destroys for ever
   And his cycle is never done.
In this room chrysanthemums and dahlias
   Like brandy hit the heart; the fire,
A small wild animal, furthers its desire
   Consuming fuel, self-consuming.
And flames are the clearest cut
   Of shapes and the most transient:
O fire, my spendthrift,
   May I spend like you, as reckless but
Giving as good return – burn the silent
   Into running sound, deride the dark
And jump to glory from a single spark

And purge the world and warm it.
The room grows cold, the flicker fades,
    The sinking ashes whisper, the fickle
Eye forgets but later will remember
    The radiant cavalcades.
The smoke has gone from the chimney,
    The water has flowed away under the bridge,
The silhouetted lovers have left the ridge,
    The flower has closed its calyx.
The crow's-feet have come to stay,
    The jokes no longer amuse, the palate
Rejects milk chocolate and Benedictine –
    Yesterday and the day before yesterday.
But oh, not now my love, but oh my friend,
    Can you not take it merely on trust that life is
The only thing worth living and that dying
    Had better be left to take care of itself in the end?
For to have been born is in itself a triumph
    Among all that waste of sperm
And it is gratitude to wait the proper term
    Or, if not gratitude, duty.
I know that you think these phrases high falutin
    And, when not happy, see no claim or use
For staying alive; the quiet hands seduce
    Of the god who is god of nothing.
And while I sympathise
    With the wish to quit, to make the great refusal,
I feel that such a defeat is also treason,
    That deaths like these are lies.
A fire should be left burning
    Till it burns itself out:
We shan't have another chance to dance and shout
    Once the flames are silent.

xxii

December the nineteenth: over the black roofs
    And the one black paint-brush poplar
The white steam rises and deploys in puffs
    From the house-hidden railway, a northern
Geyser erupting in a land of lava,
    But white can be still whiter for now
The dun air starts to jig with specks that circle
    Like microbes under a lens; this is the first snow;
And soon the specks are feathers blandly sidling
    Inconsequent as the fancies of young girls
And the air has filled like a dance-hall,
    A waltz of white dresses and strings of pearls.
And the papers declare the snow has come to stay,
    A new upholstery on roof and garden
Refining, lining, underlining the day,
    And the sombre laurels break parole and blossom
In enormous clumps of peonies; and the cars
    Turn animal, moving slowly
In their white fur like bears,
    And the white trees fade into the hill behind them
As negroes' faces fade in a dark background,
    Our London world
Grown all of a piece and peaceful like the Arctic,
    The sums all cancelled out and the flags furled.
At night we sleep behind stockades of frost,
    Nothing alive in the streets to run the gauntlet
Of this unworldly cold except the lost
    Wisps of steam from the gratings of the sewers.
It is holiday time, time for the morning snack,
    Time to be leaving the country:

I have taken my ticket south, I will not look back,
    The pipes may burst for all I care, the gutter
Dribble with dirty snow, the Christmas party
    Be ruined by catarrh;
Let us flee this country and leave its complications
    Exactly where they (the devil take them) are.
So Dover to Dunkerque:
    The Land of Cockayne begins across the Channel.
The hooter cries to hell with the year's work,
    The snowflakes flirt with the steam of the steamer.
But the train in France is cold, the window
    Frosted with patterns of stars and fern,
And when we scrape a peephole on the window
    There is nothing new to learn;
Nothing but snow and snow all the way to Paris,
    No roast pigs walk this way
And any snatched half-hour of self-indulgence
    Is an intercalary day.
Sweet, my love, my dear, whoever you are or were,
    I need your company on this excursion
For, where there is the luxury of leisure, there
    There should also be the luxury of women.
I do not need you on my daily job
    Nor yet on any spiritual adventure,
Not when I earn my keep but when I rob
    Time of his growth of tinsel:
No longer thinking you or any other
    Essential to my life – soul-mate or dual star;
All I want is an elegant and witty playmate
    At the perfume counter or the cocktail bar.
So here where tourist values are the only
    Values, where we pretend
That eating and drinking are more important than thinking

And looking at things than action and a casual friend
Than a colleague and that work is a dull convenience
  Designed to provide
Money to spend on amusement and that amusement
  Is an eternal bride
Who will never sink to the level of a wife, that gossip
  Is the characteristic of art
And that the sensible man must keep his æsthetic
  And his moral standards apart –
Here, where we think all this, I need you badly,
  Whatever your name or age or the colour of your hair;
I need your surface company (what happens
  Below the surface is my own affair).
And I feel a certain pleasurable nostalgia
  In sitting alone, drinking, wondering if you
Will suddenly thread your way among these vulcanite
    tables
  To a mutually unsuspected rendezvous
Among these banal women with feathers in their hats and
    halos
  Of evanescent veils
And these bald-at-thirty Englishmen whose polished
  Foreheads are the tombs of record sales;
Where alcohol, anchovies and shimmying street-lamps
  Knock the stolid almanac cock-a-hoop,
Where reason drowns and the senses
  Foam, flame, tingle and loop the loop.
And striking red or green matches to light these loose
  Cigarettes of black tobacco I need you badly –
The age-old woman apt for all misuse
  Whose soul is out of the picture.
How I enjoy this bout of cynical self-indulgence,
  Of glittering and hard-boiled make-believe;

The cynic is a creature of over-statements
    But an overstatement is something to achieve.
And how (with a grain of salt) I enjoy hating
    The world to which for ever I belong,
This hatred, this escape, being equally factitious –
    A passing song.
For I cannot stay in Paris
    And, if I did, no doubt I should soon be bored
For what I see is not the intimate city
    But the brittle dance of lights in the Place de la
        Concorde.
So much for Christmas: I must go further south
    To see the New Year in on hungry faces
But where the hungry mouth
    Refuses to deny the heart's allegiance.
Look: the road winds up among the prickly vineyards
    And naked winter trees;
Over there are pain and pride beyond the snow-lit
    Sharp annunciation of the Pyrenees.

xxiii

The road ran downhill into Spain,
  The wind blew fresh on bamboo grasses,
The white plane-trees were bone-naked
  And the issues plain:
We have come to a place in space where shortly
  All of us may be forced to camp in time:
The slender searchlights climb,
  Our sins will find us out, even our sins of omission.
When I reached the town it was dark,
  No lights in the streets but two and a half millions
Of people in circulation
  Condemned like the beasts in the ark
With nothing but water around them:
  Will there ever be a green tree or a rock that is dry?
The shops are empty and in Barceloneta the eye-
  Sockets of the houses are empty.
But still they manage to laugh
  Though they have no eggs, no milk, no fish, no fruit, no
    tobacco, no butter,
Though they live upon lentils and sleep in the Metro,
  Though the old order is gone and the golden calf
Of Catalan industry shattered;
  The human values remain, purged in the fire,
And it appears that every man's desire
  Is life rather than victuals.
Life being more, it seems, than merely the bare
  Permission to keep alive and receive orders,
Humanity being more than a mechanism
  To be oiled and greased and for ever unaware
Of the work it is turning out, of why the wheels keep turning;

Here at least the soul has found its voice
Though not indeed by choice;
    The cost was heavy.
They breathe the air of war and yet the tension
    Admits, beside the slogans it evokes,
An interest in philately or pelota
    Or private jokes.
And the sirens cry in the dark morning
    And the lights go out and the town is still
And the sky is pregnant with ill-will
    And the bombs come foxing the fated victim
As pretty as a Guy Fawkes show –
    Silver sprays and tracer bullets –
And in the pauses of destruction
    The cocks in the centre of the town crow.
The cocks crow in Barcelona
    Where clocks are few to strike the hour;
Is it the heart's reveille or the sour
    Reproach of Simon Peter?
The year has come to an end,
    Time for resolutions, for stock-taking;
Felice Nuevo Año!
    May God, if there is one, send
As much courage again and greater vision
    And resolve the antinomies in which we live
Where man must be either safe because he is negative
    Or free on the edge of a razor.
Give those who are gentle strength,
    Give those who are strong a generous imagination,
And make their half-truth true and let the crooked
    Footpath find its parent road at length.
I admit that for myself I cannot straiten
    My broken rambling track

Which reaches so irregularly back
  To burning cities and rifled rose-bushes
And cairns and lonely farms
  Where no one lives, makes love or begets children,
All my heredity and my upbringing
  Having brought me only to the Present's arms –
The arms not of a mistress but of a wrestler,
  Of a God who straddles over the night sky;
No wonder Jacob halted on his thigh –
  The price of a drawn battle.
For never to begin
  Anything new because we know there is nothing
New, is an academic sophistry –
  The original sin.
I have already had friends
  Among things and hours and people
But taking them one by one – odd hours and passing
    people;
  Now I must make amends
And try to correlate event with instinct
  And me with you or you and you with all,
No longer think of time as a waterfall
  Abstracted from a river.
I have loved defeat and sloth,
  The tawdry halo of the idle martyr;
I have thrown away the roots of will and conscience,
  Now I must look for both,
Not any longer act among the cushions
  The Dying Gaul;
Soon or late the delights of self-pity must pall
  And the fun of cursing the wicked
World into which we were born
  And the cynical admission of frustration

('Our loves are not full measure,
   There are blight and rooks on the corn').
Rather for any measure so far given
   Let us be glad
Nor wait on purpose to be wisely sad
   When doing nothing we find we have gained nothing.
For here and now the new valkyries ride
   The Spanish constellations
As over the Plaza Cataluña
   Orion lolls on his side;
Droning over from Majorca
   To maim or blind or kill
The bearers of the living will,
   The stubborn heirs of freedom
Whose matter-of-fact faith and courage shame
   Our niggling equivocations –
We who play for safety,
   A safety only in name.
Whereas these people contain truth, whatever
   Their nominal façade.
Listen: a whirr, a challenge, an aubade –
   It is the cock crowing in Barcelona.

xxiv

Sleep, my body, sleep, my ghost,
  Sleep, my parents and grand-parents,
And all those I have loved most:
  One man's coffin is another's cradle.
Sleep, my past and all my sins,
  In distant snow or dried roses
Under the moon for night's cocoon will open
  When day begins.
Sleep, my fathers, in your graves
  On upland bogland under heather;
What the wind scatters the wind saves,
  A sapling springs in a new country.
Time is a country, the present moment
  A spotlight roving round the scene;
We need not chase the spotlight,
  The future is the bride of what has been.
Sleep, my fancies and my wishes,
  Sleep a little and wake strong,
The same but different and take my blessing –
  A cradle-song.
And sleep, my various and conflicting
  Selves I have so long endured,
Sleep in Asclepius' temple
  And wake cured.
And you with whom I shared an idyll
  Five years long,
Sleep beyond the Atlantic
  And wake to a glitter of dew and to bird-song.
And you whose eyes are blue, whose ways are foam,
  Sleep quiet and smiling

And do not hanker
  For a perfection which can never come.
And you whose minutes patter
  To crowd the social hours,
Curl up easy in a placid corner
  And let your thoughts close in like flowers.
And you, who work for Christ, and you, as eager
  For a better life, humanist, atheist,
And you, devoted to a cause, and you, to a family,
  Sleep and may your beliefs and zeal persist.
Sleep quietly, Marx and Freud,
  The figure-heads of our transition.
Cagney, Lombard, Bing and Garbo,
  Sleep in your world of celluloid.
Sleep now also, monk and satyr,
  Cease your wrangling for a night.
Sleep, my brain, and sleep, my senses,
  Sleep, my hunger and my spite.
Sleep, recruits to the evil army,
  Who, for so long misunderstood,
Took to the gun to kill your sorrow;
  Sleep and be damned and wake up good.
While we sleep, what shall we dream?
  Of Tir nan Og or South Sea islands,
Of a land where all the milk is cream
  And all the girls are willing?
Or shall our dream be earnest of the real
  Future when we wake,
Design a home, a factory, a fortress
  Which, though with effort, we can really make?
What is it we want really?
  For what end and how?
If it is something feasible, obtainable,

Let us dream it now,
And pray for a possible land
   Not of sleep-walkers, not of angry puppets,
But where both heart and brain can understand
   The movements of our fellows;
Where life is a choice of instruments and none
   Is debarred his natural music,
Where the waters of life are free of the ice-blockade of
      hunger
   And thought is free as the sun,
Where the altars of sheer power and mere profit
   Have fallen to disuse,
Where nobody sees the use
   Of buying money and blood at the cost of blood and
      money,
Where the individual, no longer squandered
   In self-assertion, works with the rest, endowed
With the split vision of a juggler and the quick lock of a
      taxi,
   Where the people are more than a crowd.
So sleep in hope of this – but only for a little;
   Your hope must wake
While the choice is yours to make,
   The mortgage not foreclosed, the offer open.
Sleep serene, avoid the backward
   Glance; go forward, dreams, and do not halt
(Behind you in the desert stands a token
   Of doubt – a pillar of salt).
Sleep, the past, and wake, the future,
   And walk out promptly through the open door;
But you, my coward doubts, may go on sleeping,
   You need not wake again – not any more.
The New Year comes with bombs, it is too late

To dose the dead with honourable intentions:
If you have honour to spare, employ it on the living;
　　The dead are dead as Nineteen-Thirty-Eight.
Sleep to the noise of running water
　　To-morrow to be crossed, however deep;
This is no river of the dead or Lethe,
　　To-night we sleep
On the banks of Rubicon – the die is cast;
　　There will be time to audit
The accounts later, there will be sunlight later
　　And the equation will come out at last.